SWAMY
AND
RADHA'S
FIRST VENTURE

SWAMY AND RADHA'S FIRST VENTURE

SANGEETA BALRAM

Clever Fox® PUBLISHING
Chennai • Bangalore

CLEVER FOX PUBLISHING
Chennai, India

Published by CLEVER FOX PUBLISHING 2026

ISBN: 978-93-7500-391-5

ACKNOWLEDGEMENTS

Heartfelt thanks to my spouse, Abhishek Rhisheekesan, for sharing insights from his entrepreneurial journey, and to all the startups and enterprises I had the opportunity to work with.

This story draws inspiration from the entrepreneurial journey of every dreamer who dreams, believes, and takes the first leap. Their willingness to begin and staying the course through challenges have shaped the spirit of *Swamy and Radha's First Venture*.

PREFACE

Entrepreneurship does not always begin with big ideas or grand plans.

Sometimes, it begins with small acts of attention. With noticing what is not working. With wondering why effort sometimes leads to waste. With caring enough to believe that even small things can be made better.

Swamy & Radha are now a team. They are not initially trying to start a venture. They are trying to observe, learn, and understand.

Guided gently by their Thatha, and shaped by the people around them, Swamy & Radha learn to observe before acting. They listen, ask questions, and try to see the world from another person's place. This story is about learning from what does not work as much as from what does. And about understanding that the best solutions are built with people, not just for them.

Along the way, Swamy & Radha begin to see that data is not just numbers or charts. It lives in everyday patterns—in the quiet improvements that come from thoughtful, community-enabled change.

Swamy and Radha's First Venture shows how change often begins early, with attention to what is close at hand.

Sometimes, it begins with something very small— a wilted carrot, a curious mind, and the courage to ask a better question.

NOTE TO PARENTS AND EDUCATORS

This book is written with a simple belief: children learn best when ideas grow out of real life.

Swamy and Radha's First Venture introduces young readers to entrepreneurial, marketing, and design thinking ideas not through definitions, but through story. Concepts such as empathy, observation, experimentation, iteration, and community-building are woven naturally into the narrative, allowing children to understand them intuitively. Each chapter unfolds a core lesson from the entrepreneurial journey, tracing the path from opportunity recognition to branding through engaging storytelling.

The book is part of the *Swamy and Data* series. In *Swamy and Data*, Swamy learns how to observe patterns; in *Swamy and Radha's First Venture*, Swamy and Radha together learn how to design and deliver solutions.

The story encourages:

Empathy before problem-solving, Curiosity over quick answers, Learning through trial, error, and reflection, Seeing value in simple, sustainable solutions and Collaboration and teamwork. There are no perfect heroes and no instant victories. Progress is shown as gradual, thoughtful, and shared. This makes the story especially suitable for discussions at home or in classrooms—about decision-making, and how knowledge can be applied meaningfully to everyday problems.

Parents and educators may choose to:

- Pause and discuss Swamy & Radha's choices and observations
- Encourage children to notice small problems in their own surroundings and look for plausible community-based solutions
- Connect the story to basic ideas of science, data, or sustainability

Above all, this book hopes to leave young readers with quiet but powerful ideas:

that observing their surroundings, caring deeply, and trying thoughtfully are skills that matter—and can be practised early.

CONTENTS

CHAPTER 1

THE CALL OF THE VEGETABLES!: OPPORTUNITY RECOGNITION

It was a lazy, dusty Sunday afternoon at Gatinaadu, and Swamy and Radha were seated cross-legged on the cool old verandah with red-oxide flooring. Swamy flipped open his diary, its pages curled from the summer heat. He read about the lessons he had learned from Thatha—how data could be everywhere: in the way people worked, in patterns of rain, and in the small problems of everyday life.

Suddenly, from the corners of the street came Gopi Anna's loud calls,

"Carrots, Potatoes, Beans," his steady voice under the summer sun shaped by years of resilience and hard work from selling vegetables.

From behind the kitchen sink, amidst the gush of running water, Amma called out, "Swamy, buy me 500 gms of carrots. Here, take Rs. 25."

Swamy hurried to Amma, picked up a paper bag, clenched the money in his fist, and ran towards Gopi Anna.

Drenched in sweat under the scorching sun, Gopi Anna handed him the bag of carrots. Swamy rushed to Amma and handed it to her. She shook it gently and peered inside. Some carrots in the bag were muddy. Some were wilted. Some were fresh.

"Most of these carrots are not fresh," remarked Amma from behind the kitchen window.

"What to do, madam?" Gopi Anna replied. "These days, because of heavy rains, we are unable to get fresh produce from the fields. Conditions are only going to worsen, with rains wreaking havoc on most of our crops."

This baffled Swamy and Radha.

They exchanged anxious glances and scurried to Thatha to explain the impending problems that food in Gatinaadu was about to face.

Thatha lowered his newspaper and said calmly, "To find a good solution, we must first understand the pain points. And to understand pain points, we need to understand people. That means putting ourselves in their shoes."

"What are these pain points?" Radha asked.

"Sounds like something painful." Swamy remarked playfully.

Thata laughed. "Very close Swamy!." He continued. "Pain points are parts of a system that cause problems or obstructions.

Here, the key pain point is rain—but that is not in our control. Can we think of other pain points in the vegetable-selling process that can be brought under our control?"

Swamy and Radha paused. They decided to return to Thatha's question after thinking for a bit and doing some research.

That afternoon, Swamy noted in his small diary, "Good solutions begin with understanding the right problem. And to understand a problem, we must learn to feel what others feel."

He then connected it to the data lessons he was learning from Thatha and murmured to himself, "Data is indeed everywhere. It's not only in computers or charts. It's in the way vegetables stay fresh, in the hours Gopi Anna spends plucking and sorting them, and in the losses he faces when they spoil. If I pay close attention, measure carefully, and test ideas, I can use data to help people."

Radha nodded.

"So this is our first test?"

Swamy smiled and spoke with a sense of growing confidence.

"Yes! We observe, we record, we test, and we improve. That's data and problem-solving in action—right here at Namma Veedu in Gatinaadu!"

CHAPTER 2

IN ANOTHER PERSON'S CHAPPALS: CUSTOMER DISCOVERY

That dusk, Swamy and Radha sat on the bench, watching the sun set. Birds chirped as they flew back to their sanctuaries, while the sky was filled with long streaks of reddish orange. A cool breeze from the river brushed softly against their faces.

Swamy's thoughts drifted to Gopi Anna—and to how, rain or shine, he continued to sell vegetables every day.

"Surprising, isn't it?" Swamy said to Radha. "All of Gopi Anna's hard work is going down the drain because of this rain. There should be some way to ensure that the people of Gatinaadu receive good produce, and that vendors like Gopi Anna also do not suffer losses." He wondered aloud.

The next morning, Swamy went to the vegetable bazaar. It was already live with sound and movement. The air smelled of fresh mint, yellow lemons and damp earth. Baskets of fruits, vegetables, flowers, and green leaves glowed under the soft morning sun, their colours bright against the dusty ground.

"Mangoes—Rs 40 a kilo, with a Rs 10 discount!" called out one vendor.

"Bananas—Rs 20 a dozen!" shouted another, his voice rising above the chatter and clatter of the crowd.

Swamy made his way through the narrow bylanes, past rustling leaves and dry wilted flowers, until he finally spotted Gopi Anna. He decided to stay with him for the entire day, quietly observing his work—from the first sale to the last call.

He observed how Gopi Anna went to the nearby fields early in the morning, plucked vegetables, sorted and inspected them, separated damaged, rotten, and overripe ones, removed debris and mud, washed them with clean water, and then drained and dried them before putting them up for sale. All these activities took hours of effort before the vegetables were finally ready.

Wanting to help, Swamy reached into a basket and began sorting quickly, placing a few carrots aside.

"Careful", said Gopi Anna, pulling his vegetable basket away. "Each vegetable is hard earned money, please sort them properly."

Hearing this, Swamy was a little more cautious than usual. He understood trust didn't come free, it had to be earned.

Slowly, he separated the bad vegetables from the good ones with greater care than before and quietly admired the effort it took to do this every single day. He began to understand the tireless toil and hard work that went on behind the scenes.

"Here, Gopi Anna. These vegetables can now be put up for sale," said Swamy, wiping the sweat off his forehead.

Gopi Anna thanked him warmly and went on his way through the quaint lanes of Gatinaadu, with his rhythmic calls echoing, "Carrots, Beans, Potatoes."

Swamy looked at his muddy hands and thought,

"If one morning's work feels this hard, what would it feel like to lose everything to the rain?"

That day, he wrote in his diary:

"Empathy is perhaps the first step towards understanding the pain points. And it can only be built by putting ourselves in another person's chappals!" He smiled.

CHAPTER 3

THINKING CAPS ON: HYPOTHESIS THINKING

One damp morning, Swamy and Radha floated paper boats in the puddles outside their house, watching them wobble, spin, and race against each other. The sky was still heavy with clouds after the previous night's rain. Water lay pooled near their verandah and along the narrow bylanes of Gatinaadu, reflecting the grey clouds above.

Swamy nudged his boat with a stick and watched it spin in a slow circle. Yesterday's question drifted back to him.

What would Gopi Anna sell today if the heavy rains had washed away his crops yesterday?

"Radha," Swamy said suddenly, "let's think this through."

They ran inside to the small whiteboard in their study room and began brainstorming, the marker squeaking softly as it moved.

Radha tapped the marker thoughtfully. "Thatha always says the rains are not in our control. So… what is?"

Swamy paused. "Some things are. Gopi Anna plucks vegetables every day. What if he could store them safely for times like this?"

Radha's eyes lit up. "Like how we keep vegetables fresh in our refrigerator?"

"Exactly," Swamy said. "But a refrigerator would be too expensive. We need something affordable."

He snapped his fingers. "Let me think hard."

Suddenly a eureka moment struck him. "Hey, remember evaporative cooling from school?" He said, "Water can help keep things cool."

"Like magic!" Radha laughed.

"Like science," Swamy grinned. "What if we build a small refrigerator using that idea?"

Radha jumped. "Let's do it!"

That night, Swamy wrote in his diary:

Affordable refrigeration.

He underlined *affordable* twice.

Radha, who had been watching him think, spoke more softly this time. "But what if we fail?"

Swamy paused and then said quietly, "Umm, we try again."

"Just like entrepreneurs." Radha beamed.

CHAPTER 4

A ROUGH BEGINNING: MINIMUM VIABLE PRODUCT & EARLY ADOPTERS

Just before lunchtime one quiet afternoon, Thatha sat absorbed in his usual Sudoku, his pencil moving steadily across the grid in the local newspaper. Nearby, Amma was in the kitchen preparing *avial*, a South Indian dish made with a medley of fresh vegetables. The subtle aroma of coconut and spices slowly filled the house.

She glanced into the vegetable rack and exclaimed in frustration. "Vegetables are not fresh again," holding up a carrot and a potato. "Both of these are rotten. How will I make a good avial today?"

Swamy, who had been quietly watching, thought for a moment.

"Amma," he said, "can we maybe use the other vegetables? Or cut out the bad parts of these ones?"

Amma looked at him and smiled.

"Hmm… that's a clever idea, Swamy. We can still make a good avial if we work with what's fresh and carefully remove the rotten bits."

Swamy's face brightened.

"It's like solving a puzzle, Amma! Just like Thatha's Sudoku—sometimes you have to figure out which pieces fit best."

Thatha chuckled from his chair.

"Well said, Swamy! You're learning the art of problem-solving even from vegetables and avial."

"Hmm, problem-solving, yes, Thatha," Swamy said thoughtfully. "Radha and I have been wanting to solve a problem for Gopi Anna. As you know, his vegetables haven't been fresh lately, so we want to build a small, affordable refrigerator for him. That way, he can keep his fruits and vegetables fresh—especially on rainy days like these."

"That's a great plan, Swamy," Thatha said with a smile. "How do you want to go about it?"

"Thatha," Swamy replied eagerly, "I learnt in the science class about a method called Zeer cooling, that uses the principle of evaporative cooling. We'll research more on it to find out what it can offer. Our plan first is to visit Hari Mama, the potter, to get some clay pots. Then we'll go to the local sand shop to collect a small amount of river sand. With these materials, we'll build the mini refrigerator and show it to Gopi Anna. All expenses will come from our piggy-bank savings."

Thatha listened in quiet wonder and congratulated Swamy and Radha on their curiosity and effort.

Soon, Radha and Swamy headed out and returned with two clay pots—one bigger than the other. Carefully, they placed the smaller pot inside the larger one and filled the space between them with river sand. Slowly, they sprinkled water over the sand and covered the top of the larger pot with a wet white cloth from Amma's kitchen.

As the water trickled through the sand, a faint earthy scent rose in the courtyard.

"Petrichor!" exclaimed Swamy in excitement.

But their first experiment failed. The sand was too dry and did not absorb enough water, and the pots did not fit properly—one of them cracked under strain.

Radha looked at the broken pot and said worriedly, "I was afraid this would happen."

For a brief moment, Swamy felt the same. He tried to lighten the mood. "Looks like the pots weighed heavier than the idea," he said, though his voice lacked its usual confidence.

Thatha, who had been watching silently, smiled and stepped closer. "This is only your first attempt," he said. "Why not try again—with a better pair of pots?"

On Thatha's advice, they decided to replace the pots and try again. This time, they added more water and watched closely as the sand darkened and became wetter. Next, they placed the vegetables loosely inside the inner pot and measured the temperature.

Swamy quickly ran to Paati's cabinet and brought out a thermometer. Paati, lying on her cot, gently pointed to him in the right direction. "The thermometer is on the top right shelf." She said. Paati always kept her first-aid kit ready for all kinds of emergencies!

Swamy then asked Amma to place some fresh vegetables inside and noted how long they lasted at room temperature compared to inside the mini refrigerator. He drew a small table in his diary:

Vegetable | Extra Days of Freshness

Carrots | 7–10

Beans | 4–6

Potatoes | 10–14

"That's quite a few extra days!" Swamy thought, smiling to himself. "If I keep noting this every day, I'll know which vegetables last longer—and maybe even figure out how to store them better."

After two weeks of trial, error, and testing the prototype at home, Swamy and Radha decided it was time to inform Gopi Anna about their solution. The process hadn't been easy at first, but through multiple iterations, and staying with the problem they slowly arrived at a prototype that felt just right.

At first, Gopi Anna looked unsure. But after seeing the mini refrigerator in action, he nodded with approval and agreed to start using it to store his fresh produce.

"How much does it cost?" he asked cautiously.

"It's free for you," Swamy replied with a bright smile.

Overjoyed, Gopi Anna carefully arranged his vegetables inside the refrigerator and placed it on his cart, confident they would stay fresh for longer. Amma, too, was delighted—finally, she could make her favourite avial with fresh, crisp vegetables every time.

Swamy added a note to his diary:

Big steps start small.

Thatha stepped in, his voice calm and thoughtful, suggesting that early adopters be offered free trials to help them embrace the change.

By now, without even realizing it, Swamy and Radha were applying the principles of design thinking—first empathizing with a real need, then ideating solutions, building a prototype, and testing it with their first user, Gopi Anna.

CHAPTER 5

FROM CLAY POTS TO COMMUNITY: ROLES & TEAM STRUCTURE

Gopi Anna now went through the streets of Gatinaadu with his vegetables stored safely in the mini refrigerator. Before long, word about the little cooler began to spread. Other vegetable vendors noticed how fresh Gopi Anna's produce remained, and many approached Swamy and Radha, curious to learn how they too could use this simple, homegrown technology.

Swamy felt a growing sense of pride. His idea was helping others. Soon, more and more requests for the refrigerator began to come in. After some thought, they decided to give their cooler a name: **NeerMini**.

Thatha often said that the positioning of a product was just as important as the product itself—the name had to tell a story. *Neer*, meaning water in Sanskrit, felt just right: simple, rooted, and meaningful. After all, their cooler worked on the timeless principle of evaporative cooling, where water quietly did the hard work of keeping things fresh. *Mini*—because it was small, simple, and useful.

Eager to find a way to meet the growing demand, Swamy and Radha hurried to Thatha for advice.

"Thatha," Swamy said, "so many vendors want NeerMini, but we have limited budget and experience. How can we help everyone?"

Thatha who was sitting on his rocking chair in the courtyard, with a twinkle of wisdom in his eyes, replied, "What if you created a common storage space for all the vendors—and also a marketplace where they could sell their vegetables?"

Swamy's eyes sparkled. "That's a great idea, Thatha! But… how do we go about it?"

"We'll need a big NeerMini," Swamy said thoughtfully, "or maybe many smaller NeerMinis. Let's work with Hari Mama to build a larger system so more and more vendors can keep their produce fresh."

Thatha nodded slowly, approving Swamy's thought. Watching them with a proud smile, Thatha offered one final suggestion. "Why don't you divide your work? Swamy, you can focus on designing and improving NeerMini. Radha, you can work closely with the vendors—helping them store and sell their produce at a lower cost."

Swamy and Radha nodded eagerly. With clear roles and a shared vision, their small idea was ready to grow into something much bigger—something that could help the whole village thrive.

Excited, Swamy and Radha rushed to Hari Mama and shared their plan. Together, they began brainstorming and sketching ideas for a larger NeerMini system—one that could serve the entire marketplace.

CHAPTER 6

NEERMINI EXPANDS TO NEERMAX: SCALING

With their roles clearly defined, Swamy and Radha dived into work without delay. Swamy began sketching a larger Neer system, which he named **NeerMax**. He filled his small diary with design after design, tearing out pages that didn't quite match his vision.

After many iterations and discussions with Hari Mama, Swamy finally arrived at the NeerMax design: clusters of two larger clay pots nested together, with sand filling the gaps between them. These clusters could store a wider variety of vegetables in larger quantities.

Hari Mama carefully shaped the pots, ensuring they were sturdy enough to withstand the changing seasons. Each NeerMax—made up of clusters of NeerMinis—was placed in a shaded corner of the marketplace. Though sharing the same space, every unit functioned independently, running its own sand-and-water evaporative cooling system. Each NeerMax had clusters of two large pots, each unit with a separate sand layer, watering setup and a clean wet cloth covering it.

At first, finding space for dozens of units was a challenge. Eventually, they discovered a quiet, shaded spot under the big banyan tree next to Ramu's store—a perfect location for the setup.

Meanwhile, Radha went from vendor to vendor across the village, demonstrating how NeerMax could keep vegetables fresh for several extra days and reduce waste. She also introduced the idea of a shared storage system in the marketplace, where vendors could safely store produce for a small, affordable fee.

In one such vendor interview, Radha approached Rajashree Akka and asked, "Would you like to save your vegetables from this rain? We have a solution called NeerMax—would you like to try it?" Initially hesitant, Rajashree Akka agreed to test it for a few days. To her delight, her vegetables stayed fresher than ever. Gradually, other vendors joined in after seeing the results firsthand.

Word spread quickly. Vendors who were once skeptical now witnessed the benefits: baskets of carrots, beans, and potatoes stayed plump and vibrant, attracting more customers than ever. Slowly, the marketplace began to transform, one fresh vegetable at a time.

CHAPTER 7

THE PRICE PUZZLE: REVENUE MODEL CLARITY

By now, Radha had taken over as the key operations lead for NeerMax. One of her most important responsibilities was to clearly communicate the fee vendors would need to pay to keep their vegetables fresh inside NeerMax. To arrive at a sustainable and practical pricing, Swamy and Radha needed a solid plan. Since Swamy had been taking classes in Data and Statistics with Thatha, he decided to seek his advice on determining the right price point.

It was a pleasant summer afternoon, and Thatha was resting on a jute mat under the mango tree. Swamy sat beside him and asked, "Thatha, how do we know how much to charge our vendors to keep their vegetables inside NeerMax?"

Thatha thought for a moment and then asked, "Do you know how much it has cost to build NeerMax so far?"

Swamy dashed into his room and returned with his diary, its pages crammed with scribbled math. Opening it, he read aloud what he had noted:

"Large outer clay pot: approximately Rs. 400 – Rs. 800

Smaller inner clay pot: approximately Rs. 300 – Rs.600

River sand for filling: a very small amount per unit, about Rs. 100

Watering system: almost free— a few water buckets for each set-up

White Cloth for covering the top: approximately Rs. 100"

So, the total cost of building a two–clay-pot NeerMax unit is approximately between Rs. 900 and Rs. 1,600. And we have built nearly 12 of them."

Thatha then added, "If we assume the clay pots will last for about 12 months, we can spread this cost across the year."

Thatha continued. "Good. Now tell me—how many vegetable vendors have signed up so far?"

Swamy turned to Radha, who was carefully noting her conversations with vendors in her diary.

"Ten vendors so far," Radha replied.

"With that," Thatha said, "let's calculate. If we take the higher cost to be safe—Rs. 1,600 per unit—and multiply it by 12 units, the total investment comes to Rs. 19,200."

He explained, "Now spread this cost over 12 months. That comes to Rs. 1,600 per month. Divide that among 10 vendors, and each vendor pays Rs. 160 per month."

"When you divide Rs. 160 by 30 days," Thatha said with a smile, "it comes to just Rs. 5.33 per vendor per day. We can round it off to Rs 6 per day, and take the higher side. "

"On top of this," he mentioned, "you can include another Rs. 5–7 per day per vendor to cover water, and a small surplus. That extra amount will also help you slowly build more NeerMax units in the future. So in total, you can charge around Rs. 11–13 per vendor per day."

A wave of excitement washed over Swamy and Radha. At last, their confusion about pricing was gone. They thanked Thatha with bright smiles and hurried back to carefully note these calculations in their diaries.

CHAPTER 8

FRESHNESS YOU CAN SEE:
GO-TO-MARKET STRATEGY

The rains had stopped, but their memory still lingered in the market. Spoiled vegetables meant losses—everyone knew that.

That morning, the bazaar buzzed with voices, and the sharp scent of coriander and curry leaves danced through the air. Small blackboards stood in front of the stalls, prices written in chalk, wiped and rewritten as the day unfolded.

Swamy slowly unveiled NeerMax, built to serve several vendors together, their surfaces draped with cloth for the grand inauguration.

Radha kept vegetables loosely inside NeerMax, placing the vegetables belonging to each vendor in a separate NeerMax unit, careful not to mix produce from different vendors. Twelve NeerMax units meant twelve vendors could be supported. So far, ten vendors had signed up, and two NeerMax units were still free to use for the newcomers.

At first, a few vendors began arguing over space inside NeerMax.

"I came earlier today," one insisted.

"But my vegetables will spoil faster," another said anxiously.

Radha stepped in and looked at the NeerMax units carefully. "There is space for everyone," she said calmly. "If more vendors sign up, we'll rotate the storage. No one will lose out."

The murmurs slowly softened.

"Let's label them clearly, so vegetables don't mix up." she added, tying tags to each bundle of vegetables.

Vegetables from Vendor 1 – Stored in NeerMax 1

Vegetables from Vendor 2 – Stored in NeerMax 2

A nearby vendor who wasn't using NeerMax frowned. "Why show the tags?"

Thatha, who had come to witness the unveiling of NeerMax, replied calmly, "Because when freshness is visible, it attracts more customers."

NeerMax made this possible. Since the vegetables stayed fresh longer, Swamy and Radha could afford to be transparent. Customers touched the coriander leaves and the plump tomatoes, vibrant in their fresh green and juicy red hues, surprised that they hadn't wilted overnight.

"They don't smell stale," one lady said, smiling.

This assurance grew slowly, and NeerMax helped it take root.

It didn't just cool vegetables—it cooled vendors' and customers' doubts as well.

CHAPTER 9

SELLING TOGETHER: PLATFORM THINKING

NeerMax was never meant for just one stall.

Soon, neighboring vendors who weren't using NeerMax earlier began adopting it for their storage too. Since demand grew, a small design change was needed. NeerMax now had compartments divided by bamboo inserts, clearly marking the spaces for each vendor within a unit. Each vendor now paid a small daily fee. Radha suggested a simple rule: every vendor using NeerMax would place a small sign at their stall:

"Freshness Preserved in NeerMax – Community Cooling"

Then, something interesting happened.

Customers began moving from one NeerMax stall to another. They believed the system, not just the seller. Vendors, too, began to change how they worked. They started coordinating—deciding who stored what, who needed more space, and whose vegetables sold faster.

When Radha spoke to the vendors, she learned that this shift had not been easy at first.

One vendor told her,

"Coming together wasn't simple. At first, everyone was only thinking about how it would help them individually. But once we saw that storing vegetables fresh for longer helped all of us sell better, we agreed to work together."

Radha noted this carefully in her diary.

She realized something important: **shared benefit had turned silos into cooperation.**

This was community-enabled marketing.

Instead of working alone, vendors grew together. NeerMax created a shared freshness brand across the market. Losses reduced. Prices steadied. Trust multiplied.

Swamy finally understood what Thatha had meant long ago.

"A good product helps one seller," Thatha said.

"A community product builds a market."

NeerMax was no longer just a fridge. It was a platform.

CHAPTER 10

WHEN NEERMAX BECAME A BRAND:

BRANDING

The NeerMax cluster stood tall under the banyan tree, with a cool pleasant breeze surrounding it. Sun-dappled leaves fluttered above, while the soft trickle of water through the sand lent an earthy perfume, quietly adding to the rhythm to the buzzing market.

At first, it was just a name painted neatly on the side of a large clay and sand structure. People knew it as that cooling box built by Swamy & Radha. Nothing more.

But brands are not just built by paint or slogans.

They are built by what people begin to expect.

Every morning, Swamy unlocked NeerMax before the market filled. Vegetables inside still carried the smell of the field, not the heaviness of storage.

Radha noticed something small but significant. Customers had stopped asking,

"Is this fresh?"

Instead, they asked,

"Was this kept in NeerMax?"

That was the day she realized something had changed.

Thatha explained it simply. "A product solves a problem once. A brand solves it again and again—in people's minds. No loud promises. Just a quiet assurance."

Soon, customers began connecting dots. Vegetables from different stalls tasted similar, lasted longer at home, and spoiled less often. It wasn't the seller they remembered—it was NeerMax.

This was brand consistency at work. NeerMax delivered the same experience, every day, across many vendors.

Then came stories.

A hotel owner said his wastage reduced.

A street-food seller said his greens stayed fresh till night.

A homemaker said vegetables bought from NeerMax stalls lasted two extra days.

Radha wrote these down in a notebook. "These are not testimonials," Thatha said. "They are lived experiences."

NeerMax slowly stood for something bigger than cooling.

It stood for:

- Freshness without electricity
- Sustainable income for vendors

- Less food waste
- Shared progress

There was a clear reason behind NeerMax, and people could feel it.

One evening, as the market closed, Swamy noticed a new vendor setting up across the road. He pointed to NeerMax and asked, "Can I be part of this?"

NeerMax had become a trust symbol.

Thatha smiled. "Now you understand. A brand is not what you say it is. A brand is what the community says it is—when you're not around."

Swamy and Radha jotted notes in their diaries. "A brand grows from the people, shaped by the people, and for the people." Their eyes swept across NeerMax, the vendors and customers, all quietly celebrating the fruits of their efforts and accomplishments.

As the moon rose above the market, NeerMax hummed softly—with subtle pride and belief—while the stalls lay calm around it, and the vendors, tired yet smiling with contentment, gazed upon their happy vegetables and happy customers!.

EPILOGUE

NeerMax comes a full circle

The sun was setting over Gatinaadu, painting the streets golden and casting tall shadows from the stalls. Swamy unlocked NeerMax and surveyed inside. The vegetables gleamed—crisp carrots, firm beans, vibrant tomatoes—just like the first day he had helped Gopi Anna.

A little boy tugged at his sleeve. "Can my amma's vegetables stay fresh like these?"

Swamy smiled. He remembered the first wilted carrot that had sparked everything. One small question, one small act of care, had grown into something bigger than he had imagined.

Around him, the market pulsed with the footsteps of the crowd. Vendors checked their crates, placing their produce carefully inside NeerMax. Customers touched leaves, smiled at ripe plump tomatoes, and believed in a system, not just a seller. Where there had been waste, now there was value. Where there had been doubt, now there was assurance. Where there had been silos, now there was community.

Radha whispered, "It all started with noticing a problem…"

Thatha's gaze brightened with insight as he added, "And curiosity, empathy, problem-solving and persistence turned it into long-lasting change."

Swamy and Radha looked around—the younger children learning by watching, the vendors coordinating, the vegetables shining in their shared cooler. They realized something: the smallest problems and solutions can grow into the biggest changes. These tiniest acts of care can ripple outwards, touching lives far beyond what we can imagine.

Swamy and Radha now saw more patterns and possibilities, and somewhere between observation and action, they had become creators.

And for the first time, Swamy and Radha felt it fully: the surroundings could be made better, not by grand plans but with a little ingenuity, care and thoughtful action — one wilted carrot at a time.

And as the market lights flickered on, their next idea was already brimming.